Pups Have Fun

Written by Rainy Bausal
Illustrated by Peter Grosshauser

Scott Foresman

Pups like to run.

Pups can have fun.

One pup is big.

Two pups are little.

A little pup can play, and

a big pup can drink.

Here is the pup in the
big red hat.

Pups can have fun all day.

Big or little, pups like to play.

Day is done.

Pups have had fun.

High-Frequency Words: little, have,
like, is, a, can, the, big, in

Editorial Offices
Glenview, Illinois • Parsippany, New Jersey • New York, New York

Sales Offices
Parsippany, New Jersey • Duluth, Georgia • Glenview, Illinois
Carrollton, Texas • Ontario, California

ISBN 0-328-02284-5

4 5 6 7 8 9 10-V003 10 09 08 07 06 05 04 03

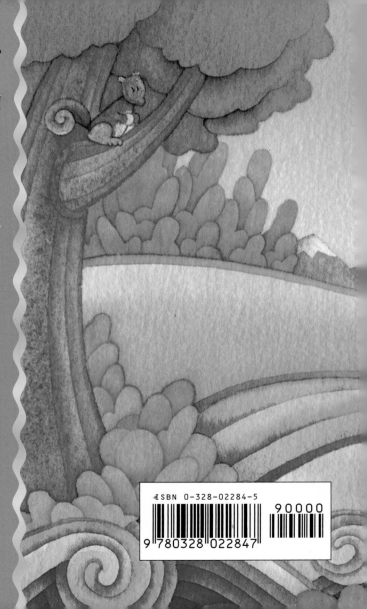

Scott Foresman
Reading

**Kindergarten
Independent Reader 23**

**High-Frequency
Words:** little, have, like,
is, a, can, the, big, in

Scott
Foresman

scottforesman.com

ISBN 0-328-02284-5

90000

9 780328 022847